Dispatches from Tumbleweed

Dispatches from Tumbleweed

Jim Stallings

iUniverse, Inc.
New York Lincoln Shanghai

Dispatches from Tumbleweed

iUniverse books may be ordered through booksellers or by contacting:

iUniverse
2021 Pine Lake Road, Suite 100
Lincoln, NE 68512
www.iuniverse.com
1-800-Authors (1-800-288-4677)

ISBN: 978-0-595-48017-3 (pbk)
ISBN: 978-0-595-60119-6 (ebk)

Printed in the United States of America

For

Kathryn & Stanley

Marriage marriage is like you say
everything everything in stereo stereo …

"Stereo"
Marriage: A Sentence
Anne Waldman

Near la frontera,
Mexicans burn fallow fields,
Smoke signals fill sky.

We landed in X,
Lost leather luggage near Y,
Never got to Z.

Good sought evil's death,
River sand swallowed spilt blood,
At last none were safe.

Mockingbird cocks eye,
Watching him sway in hammock,
Gringo with state bird.

I'm sure she's crazy,
Always moving things around,
Looking for balance.

Mondays glowed bright red,
Sanguine with restless effort,
Troops fell in trenches.

Dark mote in my eye,
Dancing like a water bug,
Shadowing the truth.

*   *   *

My mother knows you,
My father says you're no good,
My good friend Lazy.

*   *   *

Where are the mail keys?
No one answers at the post.
How can a scribe live?

Wind moans Greek chorus,
I wrap myself in towels,
Old soothsayer knocks.

I waited all night,
But you never came my way,
Dawn brought no new light.

Don't make promises,
Easy as wind in winter,
Just be your mean self.

＊　　　　＊　　　　＊

Wednesday she wore green
To show generosity
And picked my pocket.

＊　　　　＊　　　　＊

Mesquite and live oak,
Exploding with white tail deer,
Lance my heart pumping.

Old Raccoon is dead,
He lies in the greenway still,
Studied by buzzards.

Let that big rock be,
Mud slopes are too slippery,
Abandon desire.

Lying still in dark,
River rose in wild anger,
Lapping at my bed.

Let me compose you,
Made from light and love and hope,
Then my work is done.

River bell clangs cold,
Wind off Sierra Madre
Knocking at back door.

Truck blew by the house,
Throttling load through rusty gears,
Grandpa's ghost steering.

This battle with time,
Even granite loses face,
So why be ashamed?

Dawn came to the zoo,
Rock and fern dripping with fog,
Camels licked the fence.

It's all too easy,
To fool you about the truth,
But where's the pleasure?

Monotonous drone
Of small airplanes over house,
Horns of mountain monks.

Whirlwind grabs and spins,
Head and arms and feet fly high.
Now we know madness.

Here comes the news flash,
El final near, amigo,
Please, no buy in bulk.

Another lost friend,
Caught in the hell of envy,
Boiled in ambition.

We heard him snorting,
Like a wild pig in the bush,
New week same old beast.

Three colors don't rhyme,
Silver, purple & orange:
Ear jealous of eye?

Mexican fan palms,
Whispering in river air,
Stroking that old fence.

Who knocks at my door?
No one but the moth of night,
Bearing me wisdom.

She wrote her soul book,
Put in all she ever felt,
Then called it a day.

Way down on death row,
You can hear lost souls crying,
When juries go wrong.

That slippery glimpse,
Where infinity opens,
To show another.

Lost in the canyon,
We chewed insects for protein,
Mesquite beans for carbs.

Grass grows way too fast,

That's why we bought Billy Goat,

Now his beard is green.

Woke up this morning,
Don't know what to do with me,
Just lock the door tight.

Nervous as a cat,
Prancing on piano wires,
Not a chord in tune.

It wasn't my dog,
But it acted like it was,
So I let him stay.

Sunset brings dark night,
When stars sprinkle messages,
Unknown to my eyes.

Ants race along hose,
Superhighway through tall grass,
Everyone loves speed.

Yard gnome hates mowers,
Asked to live by yucca plant,
Protected by spines.

Read my lonely lips,
Porcupine muttered to skunk,
Pop stars are not us.

Hard to tell the truth,
When pain comes like bad weather,
Spoiling the picnic.

Let's take a gap year,
Four seasons doing nothing,
Our minds in neutral.

The main chance, my dear,

Greed, ambition, suit you well,

Luck is everything.

We need a locksmith,
Too many guests with worn keys,
Doors groaning open.

Crepe myrtle blooming,
Grackles squeal short wave static,
Night folds around us.

Frogs love cooling rain,
Toads prefer hot humid nights,
Bugs sing both to sleep.

At the end of day,
Most embrace the Land of Nod,
Their shift in Dream Land.

I've read your e-mail,
It's clear you love another,
I'm sorry for him.

Odd fellow he was,
Walking on hands feet in air,
His frown was a smile.

Woke up one morning,
With a whole new attitude,
Forgot it by noon.

Flowering trees pink,
Butterfly swarm golden brown,
White clouds single file.

Let's begin again,
Scratching at the mystery,
Tracing it in ink.

Stray cat picked our house,
Brought no luggage or I.D.,
Professional bum.

Near the waterfall,
Lives a very old poet,
Surrounded by books.

Honor the new day,
Open a vein for red ink,
Dip quill deep for truth.

She had bright red hair,
Freckles like the Milky Way,
Eyes blue as twin lakes.

Green leaf far away,
Holds a golden frog so rare,
Her future is ours.

Clouds hung to rooftops,
Hush fell over all things green,
Mating sky to ground.

His granaries filled,
Against the coming lean times,
Still his fingers drummed.

My friend the cat nap,
Dropping into blissful sleep,
Weight of world lets go.

Message on machine,
Don't worry I'm in a cab,
Leaving city now.

Good roof overhead,
Cool slab 'neath hot dancing feet,
Bring on happiness.

House of cards falls down,
Exposing flimsy technique,
Home of liars club.

Old buzzard was back,
Gnawing near the spinal chord,
My breathing shallow.

Hold firm to the ground,
Lightning only scars skin deep,
Burning sky tattoos.

He was a good man,
When he wasn't drinking hard,
But that was never.

Woodwinds show feelings,
Strings help to tell the story,
Drums time, brass color.

She lost her baby,
Before it came to her world,
Yet in dreams they meet.

Lost count of clock time,
Gave away a day for free,
Quite the plutocrat.

Cold front drops off Plains,
Wind moans at windows north side,
We sleep like fence posts.

Break up your schedule,
Astrologer said to me,
So I stayed in bed.

Stuffing news in skull,
Parade of skeletons danced,
Littering migraines.

She was always late,
Lost in a maze of mirrors,
But thrilled to see me.

Your dreaming double,
Met us at the fiesta,
Life of the party.

Survival instinct,
Old urge to stick around town,
And eat groceries.

Anger like lava,
Oozed red hot seeking revenge,
Smelting all away.

Quick swoop of shadow,
Strangled cry of tiny bird,
Hawk's dinner at dusk.

Clanking chains of love,
Watch couples dancing down road,
Joy and pain two-step.

Poet as tour guide,
Spotting ghosts near Alamo,
Suddenly speechless.

Tall grass crowds the door,
Vines wriggle through the windows,
Birds nest in bookshelves.

Thanks for stopping by,
We saw clear light round your head,
La puerta swung wide.

THE END

978-0-595-48017-3
0-595-48017-9

Printed in the United States
98343LV00007B/47/A

9 780595 480173